Echoes of Light

Echoes of Light

New Poems

Linda Principe

Full Court Press
Englewood Cliffs, New Jersey

First Edition

Copyright © 2015 by Linda Principe

All rights reserved. No part of this book may be reproduced or transmitted in any form or by any means electronic or mechanical, including by photocopying, by recording, or by any information storage and retrieval system, without the express permission of the author, except where permitted by law.

Published in the United States of America
by Full Court Press, 601 Palisade Avenue
Englewood Cliffs, NJ 07632
fullcourtpressnj.com

ISBN 978-1-938812-67-5

*Book design by Barry Sheinkopf for Bookshapers
(www.bookshapers.com)*

*Cover photograph, "Cape May Lighthouse,"
and author photograph, by Debbie Mazzei*

Colophon by Liz Sedlack

IN MEMORY OF

Dr. Charlotte Alexander,
teacher, mentor, friend,
with gratitude.

*"Find my hands
in the darkness
and if we
cannot find
the light,
we
will always
make our
own."*
— *Tyler Knott Gregson*

Preface

In the four years since the publication of *Tangible Remains: Selected Poems*, I've received many e-mails from students of colleagues kind enough to use the book in some of their classes. Always, those e-mails talk about a feeling of connectedness, the ways in which a particular poem brought back a memory of childhood, a place they lived, a person they loved. By far, though, the greatest sentiment was from a student who said he had never read poetry because he was afraid of it, that he believed one had to be a genius to decipher it. Reading my poems, he said, made him realize that poetry could actually be understandable and full of feelings he could relate to. I smiled when I read what he wrote; I am smiling now. Isn't that, after all, what poetry should do? As Charles Harper Webb says in a recent article, "poets must be skilled enough to communicate without obscurity. . .they must write, as the best poets always have, with insight, awareness, wit, imagination, passion, intense involvement with life . . .and in the knowledge that general readers are still out there, waiting for poems that speak to them, not just intellect to intellect, but human to human." Poetry, at its core, is not about the poet. It's about people.

Where *Tangible Remains* was nostalgic, this collection is perhaps more elegiac in tone. Robert Frost once said, "Like a piece of ice on a hot stove, a poem must ride on its own melting." I hope these poems melt their way into the minds and hearts of anyone with courage enough to pick up a book of poetry. In the darkest of times, there are echoes of light everywhere. Grab one, and make it your own.

—*Linda*
October 2015

Table of Contents

Light in a Jar, *1*
Re-View (I), *2*
Sliver (II), *3*
Even Trade, *4*
The Unburdening of Trees, *5*
Winter Tree, *6*
The Things We Keep, *7*
I Do Not Favor Light, *8*
A Certain Kind of Dark, *9*
Back There, *10*
Silver, *11*
One Wall or Another, *13*
Roomination, *14*
Ghosts of the Airwaves, *15*
A Better Blue, *16*
The Other Room, *17*
Thinking in Rainbows, *18*
The Sea Behind Me, *19*
Written in Blue, *20*
Memory of Wood, *21*
Outlines, *22*
Forty Years, *23*
Easy Alliance, *24*
Continental Divide, *26*
Broken Vase, *27*
That Kind of Light, *28*
Autumn Fire, *29*
Academic Poets, *30*
Between Seasons, *31*
What the Flesh Remembers, *32*
First Disavowal, *33*
Crohn's Contemplation, *34*
Windless, *36*
Pocketing the Night, *37*
Fire Through Glass, *38*
The Certainty of Mountains, 39

This Was Autumn, *40*
Distant Fields, *42*
Reversion, *43*
Echoes of Light, *44*
Different Doors, *45*
Conspiracy of Spirits, *46*
Words of the Heart, *48*
Jackhammer, *49*
Purveyor of Empty Rooms, *50*
All I Could Own, *51*
Scraps, *52*
Last Light, *53*
About the Author, *55*

LIGHT IN A JAR

Air in motion.
Electrified, it buzzes and hums with intermittent
flashes like Christmas lights.
These are fireflies,
in my day
lightning bugs.

On sweet summer nights,
the glow began at the edge of dusk,
clusters of yellow light dancing and darting,
here, then
there.

We chased them if they weren't close enough
to grab.
Cruel as it seems, now,
kids would remove the light
and stick it on their finger like a ring
until it died into darkness.

Me, I wanted more
than brief illumination.
I wanted to catch light in a jar
and did—
first time I wrote a poem.

Re-View (I)

I don't know what's tugging
at my sleeve like a fractious child,
but something is—

not an inner voice,
more a magnetic pull towards a place
I haven't set eyes on in years.

What can I find there
except shadows and memories,
fragments of myself and poems I never wrote
across the blue sky
beneath which my childhood played itself out?

Out of nowhere,
this feeling arrived like a lost letter,
calling me back without explanation.

Do I need a reminder,
a re-view of the view from the corner?
Do I need to see
the clouds in my grandmother's windows
or remember, in some palpable way,
all the eyes that watched over me,
all closed, now, forever?

I don't know what's tugging at my sleeve,
but something tells me
to pay attention
before I lose my shirt.

SLIVER (II)

I went there tonight,
followed the magnetic pull
back to my corner,
a short trip through many years.

Different, yes—
but not enough to matter or alter
the memories that line the street
like trees shedding leaves.

Water streamed down the curbs
the way it always did when it poured.
I resisted the temptation to kick it up
and watch it dissipate in the air
like so much else has.

I faced my pole and touched it,
wet beneath my fingers,
as familiar to my hand as this pen.
It was splintered, slimy, smeared in places
with red paint but still
solid, strong, standing.

I stood in the rain,
looked up at my grandmother's windows
and plucked a piece of wood off the pole—
not a splinter in my heart
but a sliver of the past.
I went there
to find the poet,
to find these words.

So here they are.

EVEN TRADE

You're right.
This is me here on these pages,
the one place I find myself
and lose myself.

I need the words,
and they need me,
perhaps the only reciprocal
unconsuming need I've known to last.

With my pen,
I can suspend time or escape it,
relive a moment or let it go.
There is no greater teacher
than the blank solitude of an empty page,
no history until I create it,
no past until I retell it,
no future until I ink it in.

This is the one thing
nothing but death can take,
the steady flame that's burned in every darkness
from one broken heart to the next,
the light my eyes hold to
as dreams die at my feet.

Even in silence,
I am a poet.
Sometimes, I forget that and lose my way,
but the trip down memory lane
reminded me of how much I loved
dancing on the wind with you back then—
and how words became the wings
I traded my skateboard for,
after all.

The Unburdening of Trees

Today,
the white world slipped out of itself,
Spring snow flying
from wires, roofs, branches
like heat-crazed menopausal women
shedding clothes.

Driving between margins
of silent, glistening woods,
I might have believed I was on some
unmapped Vermont country road,
old Robert Frost about to step out
to tell me to slow down, enjoy the view,
and, by the way,
you are annoying my little horse;
but two traffic lights and a horn
ended that reverie.

Still, it was like watching
shards of sun plummeting to earth,
each slice of snow etched orange
by the rising light of day,
the brilliant descent of winter.

For a moment,
I thought of all the people lost
these last few months,
who will not feel this sun on their faces,
and, sad, I smiled anyway,
the simple truth all around me:
that death is simply
one season slipping out of itself
and into another,
as naturally and silently
as trees unburdening themselves
in the early morning light
on an ordinary Saturday.

WINTER TREE
(For Mom, who said I should write a poem)

Fallen flakes
on a stark, bare maple,
limbs tucked in icy sleeves,
fingers spread,
against a winter sky,
tipped in white
like a child's when he discovers
frosting on a cake.

A little white can make
a big difference,
create a completely new image
and transform plain, empty branches
into pure
poet-tree.

THE THINGS WE KEEP

Spread across the table,
golden remnants;
not the first time I've had to sort
and dispose of pieces of lives.

Years away, I still see
the line of plastic bags filled
with my grandmother's clothes
by the door for Goodwill,
my first encounter with the finality
of death.
Angry, I wanted to empty them
so I could maintain the illusion
she'd be back.

Then, it was my dad's, the garage especially hard,
wondering what to keep
in case I might need it,
realizing that was everything since that's
why he kept things to begin with.

Yesterday, it was your jewelry,
most of which would go.
I recalled seeing you wear
that bracelet for a wedding,
that ring for a party,
and sad as I was,
I smiled at the realization glittering there:
We are not simply the things we leave behind.
If we are lucky,
we become someone's memories,
and those can't be bought, sold, or traded.
In the end,
we are so much more
than the things we keep;
also,
so much less.

I Do Not Favor Light

I do not favor light;
too harsh on the reality of illusions
and illusions of reality
I choose to play in and with.

I prefer darkness,
the kind that bears witness
to the birth of stars and souls like mine,
more comfortable climbing into night
than into a lover's bed I will only leave at dawn.

It's always been that way with me,
the terrain of my soul too dangerous to tread upon
even for me sometimes,
because, like ice in the sun,
I never know when the surface will give way,
and I might not choose to swim.

That's the paradox:
poetry brings up light from the depths
of the places we hide all the pieces of ourselves
from those who never knew us anyway,
but it is born in the darkness
that gives rise to stars.

I wouldn't have it
any other way.

A Certain Kind of Dark

There's a certain kind of dark—
I know you know it—
not populated by monsters or ghosts,
not heavy, but full, so full
of possibility:

a black canvas
awaiting the arrival of stars,
a black curtain
awaiting sunrise,
a black veil
awaiting a gentle hand to pull it back,
reveal the magic of discovery.

It's the dark of the deep woods
with its symphony of night,
that small space where water cascades off a ledge
and vanishes beneath a bridge.

It's the dark that precedes
a moment of greatness,
precursor to firelight
that suddenly fills a room and the eyes
across from yours.

There's a certain kind of dark—
I know you know it—
that we remember as the thing
that allows us to appreciate the stars
and turns, what would be simply darkness
into this poem
on a winter night.

BACK THERE

A twenty, a ten, and three singles
in my hand hurtle me headlong
back there
to the bloody June that left its imprint
on this money in your pocket
as the life left your body.

I held, today, the remnants of your life,
resurrected from the bowels of a warehouse
after twenty-one years—
checks, bills, credit cards,
evidence of your life
that never outweighs evidence of your death.

I came home as I did from your trial
every day for two weeks,
beaten up and beaten down,
sadness wrapped around me like a cloak.
Doors I never thought I'd enter again
opened, and just as I did then,
for you, I walked through them.
The difference is now
I know how to get back here from back there.

In one hand,
those blood-stained bills;
in the other,
the ink-stained pages I dedicated
to your memory.
I know which will prevail
when all is said and done.

SILVER
(For Vinny)

On this, your last night this side of earth,
all is silent
without and within.

I called you the silver fox,
old-school handsome, a gentleman,
a gentle man.
Your charm disarming,
your smile always genuine,
I came to rely on both
during those torturous years unwinding,
no resolution but a promise.

Our paths crossed under horrific circumstances,
yours, the first voice of the justice system I heard;
you knew no kindness would ease the anguish
and were kind anyway;
no words would comfort, but you spoke anyway
to make the silence bearable.

We spent hours in your office,
I, the secret witness who took a stand
but not the stand.
You warned me when the horrific details
were about to spill,
watched closely as I listened to them unfold,
and I knew you were there.
You hugged me off my feet
as the verdict echoed off the walls,
and your smile lit up that room,
a moment suspended in time.
You carried my words with you
until the very end,
proud of how I set you down,
the gift I gave you for the peace you gave me.
Rest easy, friend,
for you live in memory and on the pages of the story

where our lives intersected.

It is there forever,
read by people neither of us have ever met
but who remember our names,
one of which will be etched in stone
far too soon.

ONE WALL OR ANOTHER

Hauling the trash to the curb,
the winter air penetrating my jeans
transported me, without warning,
to my streets of memory and nights just like this.

Youth is immune to extremes
(image of my other self sitting in the shadows,
breath visible and rising,
laden with the alcohol that warmed me
and dulled my senses).

Some of my best moments
were solitary,
alone on the little wall
on the side of the corner house,
when no one wanted to venture out
into the shivering cold
of a trembling wind.

My teeth chattered,
my thighs felt cold and waxy
like the face of the dead grandmother
I kissed goodbye at sixteen.

I don't know what I was searching for,
what deep ache gripped me,
but for a moment, tonight,
I looked at the stars and realized
my two selves are not that different;
I am always just one sip away
from one wall or another.

Roomination

I've memorized
every room I've ever inhabited,
a story in each one unique to that space.

The rattle and heat
of my grandmother's boiler room in the basement,
bulb with hanging chain;
the acrid smell of fermented grapes
in the front room,
purple wood of the wine press,
old bottles on dusty shelves
hewn by my grandfather's hands.

We spent hours
in the room with the handmade table
long as the one in The Last Supper,
playing cards on rainy days—
no video games, no iPads,
just friends fully present with each other.

I retreated, sometimes,
to all those spooky rooms
at the top of the house
to view the rooftops of houses
I did not inhabit.

So much has changed since then,
and time has taught me this:
every room's a repository
I need only step inside
to find whatever self I want to meet again.

There's no such thing as empty rooms,
just empty hearts.

GHOSTS OF THE AIRWAVES

Music and memory,
intimate partners these two,
roads that end in the same place
no matter how hard you try
to avoid that destination.

Voices, there are, that fall
from the airwaves like ghosts.
I move fast, push the button on the radio,
and change the station.
I never want to hear, again,
Anita, Toni, or Whitney,
voices that lead
to some moment I've worked hard to forget.

Some songs become soundtracks
to events best left behind,
and some notes are better than notes
as reminders.

Music is memory
and most memories are meant
to be sung, to be heard
only once in any given lifetime.

A BETTER BLUE
(For my birthday buddy, Frank)

Sometimes the price of peace is high
and someone leaves without goodbye,
people left to wonder why
no one ever heard the sigh

that says, I'm sick of life, you see.
No longer do I want to be
prisoner of a heart not free
of sadness and futility.

When every day's perpetual night,
when there seems to be no end in sight,
and nothing makes the burden light,
sometimes the only choice is flight.

I'm sure there's time to contemplate:
Is this an act of love or hate?
a time, a place, specific date,
perhaps fulfillment of one's fate.

At base, we all are who we are.
We can run fast but never far
enough away from whatever scar
is left behind by a dying star.

The choice was not to end his days
or vanish in some smoky haze.
There was simply nothing left to say
and so he chose to fly away.

You live with what he chose to do,
and that's not fair, that much is true.
But know, in every part of you,
that he has found a better blue.

THE OTHER ROOM

White lace curtains
flutter in the breeze,
in and out like breath.

Second-story windows
attract the most amazing breezes,
summer winds heavy with honeysuckle,
autumn air rife with burning leaves.

On those nights I stayed,
I lay there, and if I was lucky,
the moon would be full
and I'd stare at it until I was back
in my grandmother's front porch,
the only other place I ever felt the breeze
on my naked skin.

In the silence of those nights,
I'd long for the moments when I'd share
that breeze with someone next to me;
in the silence of my nights with you,
I'd long for the loneliness and peace
of that other room.

Tonight, those curtains flutter in my mind,
white, like the ghost of you,
and I realize it wasn't peace I wanted back—
it was innocence,
freedom from knowing
how love could break you,
how unpoetic words could really be.

THINKING IN RAINBOWS

It wasn't unusual
for me to switch pens, mid-sentence,
from blue to red in a word.

I carried cartridges in my pockets like ammunition;
clueless, perhaps, but never inkless.

My Sheaffer fountain pens,
six of them, were with me everywhere,
plastic case, back pocket or clipped
to the cover of the notebook
with which I intended to change the world.

Such was the faith of a young poet
who knew nothing of the world
but everything about the mechanism of a moment
passing,
how time can bleed to death.

As I saw it, my purpose was to staunch the bleeding
with words,
to capture what I could of that moment, that time.

Ink after ink,
pen after pen,
I was thinking in rainbows,
writing the colors
of me.

THE SEA BEHIND ME

I hear the sea behind me,
a lover's steady breathing in the night,
comfortably consistent.

Any light on water is merely
reverberation of memory,
moonlight breaking on shores lost to storms,
never intended to wash away;
fireworks bursting, sea and sky one surface
of red, white, and blue fragmenting
on my feet like a tattered, fluid flag.

Moments are waves,
one after another,
a sequence of surrenders,
a consequence of misguided trust
in things I had no business trusting.

When I rose from the sand,
turned my back on the horizon,
and walked with you,
there was surety in the silence between us.

Years removed,
I hear the sea behind me and rise alone now,
knowing there was always one certainty—
the sound of the sea,
its coming,
its going—
not yours.

Written in Blue

When I venture
through all the pages of my life,
there's a lot to think about—

people who landed momentarily,
took off, and vanished forever,
a few who stayed between the lines
or in the margins and remain there.

I look at the voluminous binders
and wonder if that
is a life well lived or well imagined,
whether life is an adventure
or the real adventure was creating
the alternate reality that fit my dreams.

I could've had more lovers
or more broken hearts—no,
I've had enough of those,
some the result of the first,
but most self-inflicted by foolish hopes
that flew in the face of plausibility
and had no place in poems anyway.

I realize, too, despite its electronic preservation,
so much of it was written in blue—
and blue, oh blue,
can mean so many things.

Memory of Wood

This desk:
I run my fingers across the surface
as if touching a lover's face and smile.
This *was* my first lover, the place I spent
my desire and turned lonely nights
into rhyme,

this wood,
the silent keeper of my secrets,
adolescent anguish,
rainbow of inks I used to paint
a world I could tolerate.

Stains here and there bear witness
to who I was then,
to what's risen from those pools of ink.

This desk,
passed on to my aunt,
has found its way back to me,
a homecoming.
I approach it cautiously,
the way I would an old friend I haven't seen,
with faith we can connect again
on some meaningful level.

I take a deep breath
as I sit for a moment,
and whisper something akin to a prayer—
let me find here
the joy and peace I always did.
Let me find here
in this silent, familiar place
that wood has a memory and can return
me to me.

Outlines

On the carpet,
deep ridges where furniture sat,
there a dresser, here a night table—

I'm among ghosts here and know it,
recollecting the many footsteps
that followed me into this space
through changing years.

Laughter in the kitchen's
a faint echo now,
so too, the bickering in the living room
and the sound of a voice
calling me for one thing or another.
Mine is a life losing itself like a shadow
in a darkening sky.

I live in the shadows of people
that loved me and left me
with a store of memories to keep me
from starving.
But they are gone just the same
to a place beyond my words and sorrows.

What's left are these outlines
in the carpet, in my soul.
They say the outlines will disappear eventually,
and the rug will return to normal.
But nothing so laden with loss
ever regains its normalcy—and me,
I'm content with my ghosts.

Because they are already gone,
I need not survive their loss again.

FORTY YEARS
(For Debbie)

We are those Vermont skies,
ever-changing, always us.
No matter how often you watch
the heavens fade to lavender,
you never tire of the sight or fail to see
the moment is magic, even in its repetition.

We've not escaped the ravages of time,
the painful losses of growing older;
we've buried parents and friends,
lost parts of ourselves to those
who couldn't nourish our dreams
or feed our souls.

For forty years,
we've been the keeper of each other's dreams,
and when we dared go beyond
what the world wanted of us,
we were more than the sum of parts,
more than we ever believed we could be.

Bound by history, a million nameless things,
we are more each other's soul
than most of the people we know—
and that's what I see when I see Vermont—

our infiniteness in that sky full of stars,
our determination to hold to what's true
in the sight of that rickety-crickety bridge,
our steadfast faith in each other in the mountains
that have survived all the tempests,
a bit worn, a bit craggy,
but still standing and still casting
formidable shadows.

EASY ALLIANCE
(For Barry)

For years, two mornings per week,
I'd follow the lingering scent
down the corridor to the office
where you'd greet me
like a friend you hadn't seen in years.

I'd quip, *"Even your cologne is oxymoronic,
masculine-soft,"* and smile
as you threw your head back, laughing.

Ours is the easy alliance of kindred spirits,
two sides of the same coin, you said once,
to describe the you I see in me, the me I see in you,
that is us.

With you, never the need to set boundaries
or close doors,
to play hide and seek with who I am
or hope to be.
You always read my eyes
the way one might explicate a poem
and knew, before the words came,
what those words would be.

I've trusted that much of myself
with few, and you know that.
Consummate storyteller you are,
but I was a story you never tried
to change or re-write.
Through time, you've been
the best of bonds,
the simplest of affections,
the rare sensibility of two souls
comfortable in each other's presence,
even in silence.

I am grateful, friend,
for this steadfast, easy alliance
with the one guy who wrote me a poem
without ulterior motives and who is,
as he reads that last line,
throwing his head back
and laughing that laugh
that made of my mornings
a song.

CONTINENTAL DIVIDE

From across the world,
the eyes of the past arrive;
one click, and here you are
just as I remembered you.

Still no easy smile crosses your face,
like centuries of sorrow have settled there.
I see it, that pensive look,
as you stare into the distance beyond the edges
of the photo,
same way you did then.

Was that the draw?
That kinship of bearing something
we could not name but could feel
in our deepest places?

I smile at your mild reproach—
you *didn't* know I was a poet
who spent nights writing, a pity, you say,
because you loved poetry back then.

I'll never know if you'd have fallen
in love with the words that I spend my nights seducing
onto empty pages of my life,
words I have sent you now
without fear.

Maybe I simply didn't want to know
because I *did* know, even then,
that sometimes possibility just isn't enough,
that arms, loving though they might be,
do not cross continents.

Broken Vase

Once, a vase slipped from my grasp,
shattered at my feet,
pieces too numerous to count,
even as I picked them up.

Alone at a table for hours,
I matched fragment to fragment,
trying, as best I could,
to recreate something
I knew would never be whole again,
no matter how close I came
to a unified front.

I glued each piece into place,
holding tight until it stuck
and the pattern and design began to show.

When that was done,
I stood back amazed at the illusion of wholeness.
I counted on no one looking closely,
knowing no one ever does.

And so it is with me;
one close look's all it would take
to shatter the illusion and reveal
the million empty spaces where I should be.

I count on no one looking closely.

That Kind of Light

Half imagination,
half reality—
that is the space I occupy.

Sometimes, the memory of your eyes
is like staring into a deep pool,
part of you I saw, once,
there beneath the surface like a gold coin
just out of reach.

Sometimes, you feel
like the reflection of stars on black water,
an illusion so inviting it makes one
want to risk the drowning,
as if touching that kind of light
can ever be anything more than a passing moment.

I've lost track of how long I've been
caught between the lavender and blue
of twilight,
feeling and nothingness that is
like eternity when I reach into empty air.

I've got to believe
I was meant for more than yearning
and not here simply to make of the ache
a song I can never sing.

Though you are gone
like those stars on black water
that disappear at daybreak,
I need to believe that I knew, intimately,
that kind of light
for more than the simple purpose
of appreciating darkness for what it is.

AUTUMN FIRE

Autumn fire:
these trees in a row
like flaming candles against the blue.
Fall is a feeling,
not unlike the setting sun—
the most beautiful kind of dying.

They know, these trees,
about borrowed time,
that brazen, courageous orange
a last stand against the onslaught of wind
that will strip them to skeletons,
their death no more merciful
than anyone else's.

Every year, for weeks,
they move from flicker to flame,
to autumn fire,
time the accelerant that reduces them
to embers on the grass
strewn about like pages
from books we barely remember,
though we know how the story ends.

ACADEMIC POETS

I dislike a poem
that screws my brain into a ball:
obsolete words, oblique references,
academic poets who say
something impeccably important
that nobody gets.

I prefer the persistence of moment into memory,
the accessibility of a simple tree
that is simply a tree in the snow
and doesn't become a treatise
on the mechanics of a snowflake.

Give me a plain old poem,
an ordinary event in the life
of an ordinary fool I'd like to meet or be—
no footnotes,
no arcane allusions,
not something that illustrates the poet's intelligence
but rather the human heart
in all its imperfection.

Spare me your brilliance,
for Christ's sake,
and write a few lines I can read
and wouldn't mind saying I'd written.

BETWEEN SEASONS

Is there some starlit country road
I'm supposed to walk tonight,
my breath rising on cold air?

Is there some lone tree
I'm supposed to lean against,
survey a landscape caught
between seasons?

Is there a sky bursting with moonlight
I'm supposed to be sitting beneath,
strumming my guitar in search
of a love song?

Is there a pair of eyes waiting for me
to step into view
that will brighten at the sight of me
and invite me on a journey to the soul behind them?

Is there a voice waiting to spill
withheld words at my feet,
practicing how to say what's not been said
until the moment I'm there to receive it?

Is there somewhere I'm supposed to be
where the space I don't occupy matters,
where some heart feels my absence
and wishes I were there?
If I pick up my guitar, tell me,
will it take me to a country road
I'm supposed to walk
or down memory lane where my fate was clear
until the moment it escaped me?

What the Flesh Remembers

Fire of a first touch,
immediate gasp of recognition:
That is what the flesh remembers
as day breaks the sky.

The skin can feel
the soft presence of dancing fingertips,
even in,
especially in, their absence,
touch etched there like a tattoo.

Hands can retrace curves
and know them the way sculptors know
every nuance of the clay as it takes shape.
Hands have memories;
wring them, and one is bound to fall out.

Goosebumps,
like Braille for the blind heart,
rise and allow one body to read another in the dark,
every word chasing itself to a breathless destination.

What the flesh remembers is love,
plain and simple,
the splinter of it stuck in the skin
like the good hurt that it is.

FIRST DISAVOWAL

That moment approaches
like some neglected lover demanding attention,
insisting I revisit,
no matter the passing years or veil of fog
that obscures such recollection.

A doorway, black wooden door flung open,
you on the top of the step,
me below it,
my gaze fixed upward toward your face,
half in sun, half in shadow:
I hear your confession as if there is cotton
in my ears.
There isn't.

I didn't know what to make
of your expressed desire,
how to respond to your emotion, and so I didn't.
You were only the first of many.

My dying began with that first disavowal.
I lacked the courage
to validate the truth of you standing there,
in the flesh,
terrifying to my young, untutored heart.

I see you today and smile,
knowing we'd have been dangerous together—
awesome, wicked-dangerous,
if only I'd stepped up to meet you
instead of closing the door.

Crohn's Contemplation

1. Visualization

And so they tell me
to take the broken part of me
and visualize something else and replace it.

Take the places inside
where blood trickles, settling into small pools,
and transform them into streams
of clear Vermont water running smoothly
through woods and emptying into ponds.

Imagine, in the holes that fill your central core,
seeds of wild flowers
nourished by the tears that flow inward,
and see, in the eye of your mind,
gardens growing there and filling you with life.

Look at the empty pockets inside
and fill them like you did as a kid,
with candy, spare change, pretty stones
from the edge of a lake,
or worn glass stolen from the shore.

Walk headlong into the raging storm there,
the war zone,
the beast in the belly,
the giant in your gut,
and strum on strings until you either tame them
or make them dance.

Look long, look hard,
beyond reality
to places past your field of vision
and find the vision of a field—
start running and keep running
until, so filled with the freedom of the wind,
you remember the taste of a day

unblemished by illness.

Do this, some voice inside says,
because if you lose the dream to the disease
you will die
of disappointment.

2.What Lives Inside

I don't know what to make
of these snarling insides, the hissing
in the coils of my center,
or how to live inside a body devouring itself
for reasons beyond medical understanding.

No denying I own this uninhabitable disease
affected by which—
what goes in my mouth or what comes out?
It's the worst kind of fire inside,
not extinguished by drugs, release, or love,
a perpetual itch one can't scratch.
It's a gremlin gnawing,
a woodpecker slowly chipping at a tree,
or the heat of a sun rising
where it's not supposed to,
a sun with no light.
No flowers sprout in the ditches inside me,
pieces of me lost,
absences felt only by me
as I battle each day
for the strength to surpass limitation,
the simple right to live a life defined
by something more than sickness.

I remind myself
when I feel the approach of shadows
that there is much more inside than disease;
there is also poetry,
the one way to heal the part of me
beyond medicating.

WINDLESS

Chimes in a tree,
still and silent on this windless night,
remind me of rooms
right after someone leaves and emptiness
reclaims its space.

Memories shimmer at the edge
of consciousness,
threatening to reclaim *me*,
though I'm better at fighting,
still unsure of whether I'm winning or losing.

I sit in the shadows,
philosophizing about all the me's I've been,
wondering which was the one
that encompassed the best me;
damned if I know.

In the midst of this meditation,
stars seep through dark sky
like blood through a bandage
that covers but fails to hide
the wound beneath.

I see those chimes,
still and silent, and know
what it means to long for the wind,
what music awaits the touch of the breeze
to give it life.

So I rise, run my fingers
across those silvery pipes
and smile as the air vibrates with sound;
sometimes, on windless nights,
you must become the wind
to save the moment
from songlessness.

POCKETING THE NIGHT
(For T. John)

Tonight, the bay folds itself
into quiet creases that pocket the night,
as a man unknowingly
prepares to leave his ravaged body.
The soft breeze is not the shallow breath
of the dying
but the constant, steady wind
of the breathing universe.

If I guess correctly,
the tremor of this moment whispers
that tomorrow he'll be loosed from here,
and his dying will match his living—
hard, uncompromising, silent anger,
for a change.
He will go surrounded by those who loved him—
and that is from their goodness,
not from what he cultivated.

At some point,
in the approaching hours,
my best friend will cry out,
a fatherless child,
as if she hasn't done that all her life.

She will forget the father she never had;
remember only the one she got
as he lay dying
and the bay folded itself into creases,
pocketing the night
that welcomed him.

Fire Through Glass

Absolute magic,
the sight of fire through shards of glass,
clear and clean like air in winter.

Flames dance into a rainbow,
reflected through sky blue, grassy green, autumn orange,
bleeding-heart red,
a kaleidoscope of feeling.

There are stories in this container,
invisibly written on each piece—
places I've never been,
people I've never known,
memories not mine picked up on shores
I've walked,
dreams not mine written in pink
across horizons I've stood beneath
with glass in my hand
and a whisper in my heart.

Absolute magic,
the sight of fire through glass
I call Sea Lights,
irony in a jar—

I have set the sea on fire.

THE CERTAINTY OF MOUNTAINS

Cold air bites my lungs,
standing outside in the darkest dark,
inhaling deeply and suddenly aware
of what breathing is for.

I see those innumerable stars
as if seeing for the first time,
what an unhindered sky can do and be,
jewels on a necklace,
no beginning, no end.

The snap and crackle of live fire
fills the room inside with heat and shadows
I see but cannot reach
except within my mind.

The soft bed beneath me,
total soundlessness outside the windows. . .
I sleep, knowing
the dream of home is not one
I will lose on waking.

Perhaps the certainty of mountains
is the only one I will ever know.

For now,
another night passes in Vermont
as I lie here trying to conjure
the faith to believe that, down the road,
I'll be passing *every* night in Vermont
and remembering, instead,
the longing of *this* one,
as one remembers a dream.

THIS WAS AUTUMN

The smell of the air—
half-balsam, half-smoke,
nestles in my mind
like clouds hovering above mountain tops.

This was Autumn—
apple cider stand by the side of a road
where water slid down rock
and dissipated into a stream;
fresh corn blackening on a grill
beneath an October blue
that was anything but blue,
guitars riding the air
vanishing into echo.

This was Autumn—
trees on fire,
orange glory and white picket fences,
the presence of great poets
silent as inscriptions on marble.

Walking into crisp, clear air,
stars brighter than I'd ever seen,
that place, that moment
is as vivid as if I'd seen it yesterday.

But yesterday's forever away,
stores closed, cabins gone,
orange now only embers
of Autumns lived.

Sometimes, I think,
all that's left of Vermont are the memories I carry—
but then I remember
that skies may change but never leave,
wishes may die but stars twinkle anyway,
as if to say, "Whenever you're ready,
we're here,"

in the sweet place where memory and hope
intersect like two roads
you need not choose between
because both will lead you home.

Distant Fields

Buses:
Watching roads unwind as the sun set,
the descent of night was magic.
Lights twinkled in houses
on the edge of fields in the distance.
I wondered about the inhabitants,
what they'd do if a stranger, like me,
knocked on the door and said,
"What can you teach me about life?"

I lost myself staring out the window,
creating in my head
worlds I still inhabit all these miles and years
down the line.

I liked the freedom of a suitcase,
the idea of falling asleep and waking
in a different state.

Before life intervened,
I imagined myself a perpetual wanderer,
learning from the road
things home could never teach me.

Clearly, I was destined for more
than waiting on a bus stop
and simply dreaming
of distant fields?

REVERSION

I recognize the eyes,
seen nearly every day for half a century,
but the blankness there disconcerts me.
This is a different kind of death.

I can't memorialize the still living being,
find words to describe a loss,
not quite a loss,
or the empty room,
not quite empty.

She inhabits a world vastly different
from mine:
In hers, those she loved,
those I loved too, are alive—
not fleeting memories but real,
the recreation and resurrection of better times.
She's accomplished
what I strive for in so much of my poetry—
the reversion to simple joy
when life was easier and love
untainted by death.

In some way,
I don't blame her;
I wouldn't come back here either,
if I could see my grandmother's eyes
someplace other than in memory.

ECHOES OF LIGHT

Of the path I walked,
only traces of wear beneath
the green overgrowth of life passing
remain.
I stand like a poet of old
and wonder—
would I have walked it
if I'd known it ended in shadow?

Of the skies that canopied my nights,
only expansive darkness now,
as the poet I am looks up in silence
and wonders how stars
become echoes of light.

Of the passion that drove me,
the fire that fueled dreams
surrendered unwillingly to the truth,
only embers in empty rooms once inhabited by love
still glow.

I put down my pen long ago,
refusing to stir them and bring to life
a fire I can't warm myself by.
Whether that's acceptance or resignation,
I'm never sure.

Of me with you,
only remnants,
tattered ribbons in yesterday's wind
of who I was and you chose not to be,
ghosts.

Yes, I'd have walked the path anyway
because, of me, what's left,
is a soul that still finds magic
in the echoes of light where
stars used to be.

DIFFERENT DOORS

The irony does not escape me,
walking down hallways you walked,
meeting people who loved you,
primarily because they didn't know you
the ways I did.

I admit there are days
I feel you here;
that blonde aide who resembles you
dissembles me, sometimes,
when she enters the room and looks at me.

I recall, with such clarity,
your excitement as you ran to the truck
the day you got the job,
how terrified you looked your first day
as I dropped you off and watched you
walk through the same doors
I walk through, now,
several times a week.

This feels like your place and,
for the time being,
a place I need to inhabit
in a way I could never inhabit you.

I can find alternate ways to enter
the building,
but there is, I'm afraid,
no changing the exit,
yours or mine.

Conspiracy of Spirits
(For D.G.S.)

You were my history
before I knew I had one,
the one person from my earliest days
I chased in my mind
through the silence of unwinding years—
undeniably, the touchstone of my childhood.

We spent, together, all our days,
nine years of nine-to-three,
learned more from each other
than we ever did in classrooms.

How many times, with just a glance,
did we reduce each other to suppressed laughter
in the middle of religion class,
despite the threat of eternal damnation?

How many times did we fly
across that playground, Autumn leaves crunching
beneath our feet, and spin on that little green
merry-go-round, faster and faster,
half-hoping it would spin off its axis
and into some other place
where the only thing uniform
was the presence of stars?

We were never meant for restrictions,
and that's what united us, a conspiracy of spirits.
We did not want to be good girls.
We just wanted to be.

I choked on my first cigarette with you,
stole my first glance at *Playgirl* with you,
each other's steady light in the wind
long before we understood
the damage wind could do.

You were my history,
the past I chased into the present,
through timeless wondering.
Hard to explain, isn't it, the depth
of what connects us beyond the empty space
between computer screens?

WORDS OF THE HEART

You've lost before,
but not like this.
This one's a chasm so wide and deep,
you don't know how to cross it.

Try as you may to deny the truth,
it lives with you, the inarticulate ache
of a permanent, unanticipated absence.

You avert your eyes as if I won't see,
but I see more than you'd like me to,
the vacancy light once inhabited.

I could say she'd never want you
to feel this way,
that she'd be unhappy with the changes
forged in the person she knew and loved.
She would not want this for you;
of that I am sure.
But nothing I say will matter anyway.

To live with regret is to lose precious time
to what we cannot change.
You're sorry, I know,
for things you didn't say and do,
but guilty only of living,
as we all do, under the false assumption
that you had all the time in the world.

The simple truth is that we don't
and so we need to speak the words of our hearts
while they beat.

Take my hand.
I will help you cross this chasm safely
back to the you she knew and loved.
It's what she'd have wanted of you,
what she'd have expected of me.

JACKHAMMER
(For Pat)

In the hallway,
fluorescents flickering overhead,
we stood, the CT rumbling behind the door,
and wore our worry like masks.

The intonation and inflection of your voice
still visits me, along with the wistful smile
that crosses my face when I recall your words—
Concrete. Goddamned concrete—
when I expressed fear of what the head scan
might show.

We laughed aloud,
necessary comic relief in the face of uncertainty,
especially amusing to me
given you were her sister in stubbornness;
hearts of gold, heads of granite.

If I'd have known your departure
would be so sudden, years later,
I'd have thanked you then
for pacing the halls and mumbling with me,
your caring and love for her the only one,
excepting mine, I believed was genuine and unquali-
fied.

You walk with her, I know.
She's convinced the green hearts on the shore
are gifts from you,
the feather that floats to her feet
part of your wings.

While the nicety of hearts and wings
is not wasted on me,
I need something much more,
if you can manage it:

a jackhammer would be greatly appreciated.

Purveyor of Empty Rooms

Not quite grief that grips me
as I stand in the doorway looking in—
a threshold I've known far too often
in my life.

I am the purveyor of empty rooms,
not a position one ever adapts to.

One drawer at a time,
I sort through a life
that was part of my life all my life,
nearly every day.

There are no words
for that kind of absence.

Your clothes hang in the closet,
mute reminders
empty of substance,
the way I feel sometimes.
Fully aware you're not coming back,
I've still no heart to do this thing just yet.

I've watched almost all the players in my life
leave the stage,
each final exit a hole in my soul.
I've said so many silent goodbyes,
I've stopped counting.

But as I stand here,
I know that, now,
I am one goodbye from living the words
to a song I couldn't change
no matter how many times
I rewrote them.

There are no words
for that kind of truth.

All I Could Own

I watched curtains move,
long after midnight,
convinced the world breathed
through those windows,
my youthful heart howling at the moon,
only in silence because silence
was all I could own.

How could someone so close
be so out of reach?
How could I, with all my words,
not find the right ones?
This is what I'd think
as I lay there making rhymes in the night.

That was the child,
full of fire that life would extinguish,
the poet full of the forbidden;
and what the world would not allow
she created a space for in her heart and mind
where no one could touch it.
And there it still lives.

I think of those curtains,
blowing in, blowing out
on all those windows, on all those nights.

Is that world still breathing
though I am not there?

Am I?

SCRAPS

Scraps of night, of light,
of my heart on scraps of paper:

In the life of a poet,
it comes down to this: pieces of us
on pieces of paper,
scribbled here or there
in a flurry of excitement
or moment of despair.

Strung together, they're the measure of time,
dreams hung on the clothesline of passing years,
dried by the sun of another day,
drenched by the rain of memory.

How heavy the night I wrote your name,
repeatedly, on a sheet of paper,
I love you beneath it,
and recited it like a chant, like a prayer,
knowing it didn't matter;
the stars above me would never
grant that wish.

So I tore up that paper
and tossed the scraps into the air,
watched the wind scatter them
like flurries of snow and carry them off.

But they never left me,
those words, that night,
those scraps of my heart
that still float somewhere
on the winds of time
whispering your name.

LAST LIGHT

See how the sky creases
like something folding into itself,
how blue slowly surrenders to shades of gray
and clouds layer themselves like fortresses.
This, the choreography of closing day,
is a dance toward darkness
whose steps I intimately know.

The magic of this ending
is that it's temporary and will repeat itself
without taking anything when it goes
that it can't give back in the morning light.

Mesmerized, it's a show
I never weary of,
variations on a theme,
like a painting repainting itself.

See that thin line of pink
just between the gray,
above and below,
that crinkle in the fabric of sky—

that is the last light of day—
a pink place where hope resides
and poets are born.

There is no dying there.

About the Author

Linda Principe is an adjunct professor of English at the College of Staten Island, where she has taught writing and literature for the last twenty-eight years. She is also a freelance writer and editor. She is the author of *Surviving Murder: A True-Crime Memoir*, which recounts the harrowing murders of her aunt and uncle by their son, and *Tangible Remains: Selected Poems*. Writing poetry since the age of thirteen, her poems have appeared, through the years, in a variety of publications. In her spare time, she enjoys reading, playing the guitar, songwriting, and collecting sea glass.

Index of Titles

A Better Blue, *16*
A Certain Kind of Dark, *9*
Academic Poets, *30*
All I Could Own, *51*
Autumn Fire, *29*
Back There, *10*
Between Seasons, *31*
Broken Vase, *27*
Conspiracy of Spirits, *46*
Continental Divide, *26*
Crohn's Contemplation, *34*
Different Doors, *45*
Distant Fields, *42*
Easy Alliance, *24*
Echoes of Light, *44*
Even Trade, *4*
Fire Through Glass, *38*
First Disavowal, *33*
Forty Years, *23*
Ghosts of the Airwaves, *15*
I Do Not Favor Light, *8*
Jackhammer, *49*
Last Light, *53*
Light in a Jar, *1*
Memory of Wood, *21*
One Wall or Another, *13*
Outlines, *22*
Pocketing the Night, *37*
Purveyor of Empty Rooms, *50*
Re-View (I), *2*
Reversion, *43*
Roomination, *14*
Scraps, *52*
Silver, *11*
Sliver (II), *3*
That Kind of Light, *28*

The Certainty of Mountains, *39*
The Other Room, *17*
The Sea Behind Me, *19*
The Things We Keep, *7*
The Unburdening of Trees, *5*
Thinking in Rainbows, *18*
This Was Autumn, *40*
What the Flesh Remembers, *32*
Windless, *36*
Winter Tree, *6*
Words of the Heart, *48*
Written in Blue, *20*

www.ingramcontent.com/pod-product-compliance
Lightning Source LLC
Chambersburg PA
CBHW032213040426
42449CB00005B/579